TUNING IN

THE SOUNDS OF RADIO

EVE & ALBERT STWERTKA
PICTURES BY MENA DOLOBOWSKY

JULIAN Ⓜ MESSNER

Design by Malle N. Whitaker.
Manufactured in the United States
of America.

Lib. ed.
10 9 8 7 6 5 4 3 2 1
Paper ed.
10 9 8 7 6 5 4 3 2 1

**Library of Congress Cataloging-in-
Publication Data**

Stwertka, Eve.
  Tuning in: the sounds of
  radio / Eve and Albert Stwertka.
      p.   cm.—(At home with
  science)
    Includes index.
    Summary: Discusses how radio
  works, how it was developed, and
  the different ways in which it is
  used. Includes related activities.
    1. Radio—Juvenile literature.
  [1. Radio.] I. Stwertka, Albert.
  II. Title. III. Series.
  TK6550.7.S78   1992   91-16058
  621.384—dc20   CIP AC
  ISBN 0-671-69460-X (lib. bdg.)
  ISBN 0-671-69466-9 (pbk.)

CONTENTS

WIRELESS WONDER

If creatures from outer space visited our planet they would be puzzled by many things. One puzzle would surely be: What are those strange boxes that people carry around or keep at home? Voices and music come out of them. They bring news and weather reports, dance tunes, operas, political speeches, sports events, and religious sermons. How can so many different sounds be packed in one box?

You've probably guessed it. We earth people call this box a radio.

Do you think the earthling will let me keep it!?

Be careful with the little noise box!

Weird creatures!

This is my first U.F.O.!

AMAZING! It even has an antenna... just like me!

Here... Let me put the antenna up!

Before radio was invented, the only way to make sound travel very far and very fast was to use the telephone. But the sound signals sent by telephone can't travel everywhere. Telephone signals have to run through a wire, so they can only reach the places where special wires have been installed.

The sound signals of radio, on the other hand, travel freely through the air. They also fan out, or *radiate* in all directions. That is where the name *radio* came from, and that is why the radio is referred to as *the wireless* in some countries.

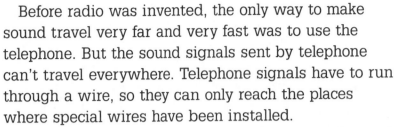

Try this...
Slowly turn the dial of your radio. Listen to each station. Make a list of all the different kinds of music, talk, and foreign languages you can hear.

6

Radio had its start in 1899, when the Italian scientist Guglielmo Marconi was able to send the first wireless signal across the waters of the English Channel. The distance was 85 miles.

That same year, a ship in the Channel was damaged by strong waves and came close to sinking. Luckily it was equipped with a wireless transmitter. Its distress signals reached the receiver station on shore, and help arrived before any lives were lost.

7

By 1901, Marconi was able to send a radio signal all the way across the Atlantic Ocean, from the coast of England to St. John's in Newfoundland, Canada. Soon, radio became the number one instrument for locating or bringing help to people in distress. For nearly a hundred years, radio signals have led rescuers to sinking ships, downed airplanes, lost expeditions, and sick people in hard-to-reach places. Not only that, but radio reports give us early warning of dangers such as storms, earthquakes, floods, and erupting volcanoes.

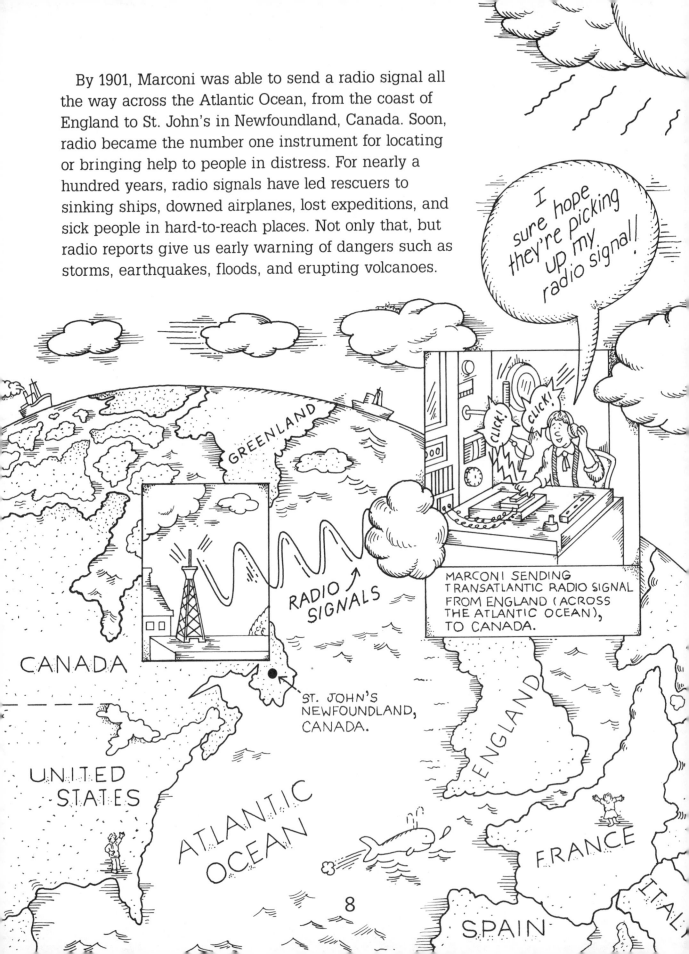

MAKING RADIO WAVES

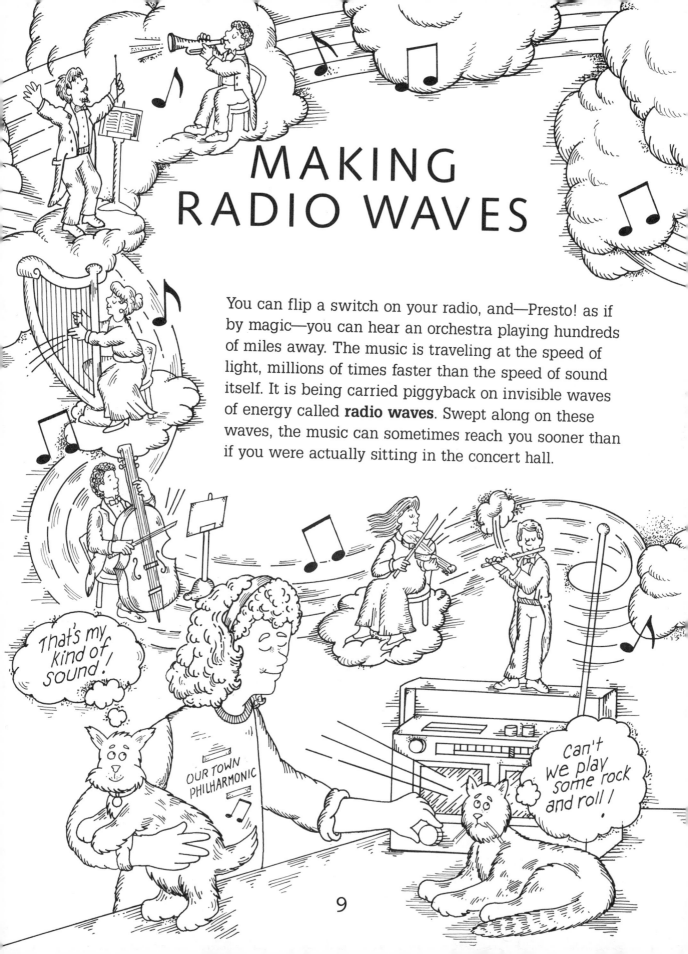

You can flip a switch on your radio, and—Presto! as if by magic—you can hear an orchestra playing hundreds of miles away. The music is traveling at the speed of light, millions of times faster than the speed of sound itself. It is being carried piggyback on invisible waves of energy called **radio waves**. Swept along on these waves, the music can sometimes reach you sooner than if you were actually sitting in the concert hall.

9

To understand how radio waves are made, think of other waves that you know about. When you drop a stone into a pond, the splash makes the water move up and down, or vibrate. You can see the vibration cause waves of water to ripple and spread out.

Radio waves are also made by vibration. But unlike the waves of the pond, radio waves are made by the vibration of tiny electric charges.

Try this...

Take a string and fasten it tightly between two supports. It should be very taut but free to move up and down. Pluck the string in the middle and watch it vibrate. You will hear the sound wave made by the vibration.

10

The electric charges that create radio waves are tiny particles called **electrons**. Electrons are among the basic building blocks that make up all matter. They move easily through wire made of copper metal.

When the wire is connected to a power supply—a battery, for example—it becomes a sort of pipe through which the electrons flow. The motion of electrons through a wire is called electricity.

Here comes the power! Let's GO!

Try this...

Buy a coil of bell wire from your local hardware store. Cut off a 3-foot piece of the wire and strip off the plastic covering from the two ends. Tape one end to the top of a flashlight battery. Tape the other end to the base of a flashlight bulb. Touch the bottom of the bulb to the top of the battery. The bulb lights up because electricity is flowing from the battery through the wire into the bulb.

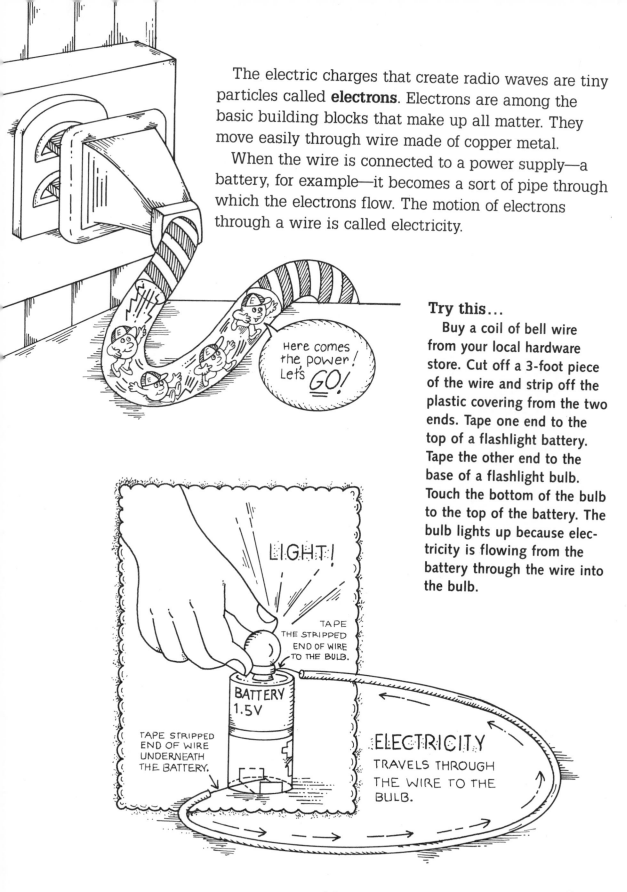

LIGHT!

TAPE THE STRIPPED END OF WIRE TO THE BULB.

BATTERY 1.5V

TAPE STRIPPED END OF WIRE UNDERNEATH THE BATTERY.

ELECTRICITY TRAVELS THROUGH THE WIRE TO THE BULB.

To produce radio waves, the broadcasting station causes electrons to vibrate back and forth in a wire. This wire is called the transmitting **antenna**, because it transmits, or sends out, radio waves. The waves radiate out in every direction. They can travel through air, or wood, or the brick walls of a building. They even go through your body without your feeling anything.

Like all waves, radio waves carry energy. This means that the waves can make something move, even at a distance.

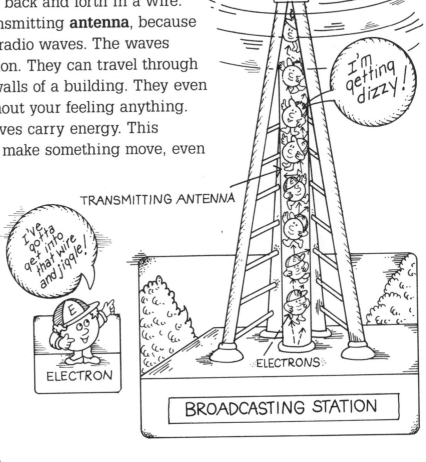

Try this...

Float a cork on a basin of water. Then drop a marble or a coin into the basin. Notice that the waves spreading from the splash have the energy to move the cork up and down.

12

When ocean waves damage a boat in a storm, it's easy to see that the moving water carries a great deal of energy. It is harder to imagine the energy carried by radio waves because nothing seems to be moving. Actually, though, the transmitting antenna is radiating powerful electric energy. This energy is so powerful that it can move the electrons in another antenna located a long distance away. The electrons in this receiving antenna follow the motions of the electrons in the transmitting antenna exactly. They copy the signals they receive like partners in a dance. The power to transmit the electron dance is what makes radio possible.

The faster electrons vibrate, the more waves are sent out every second. The number of waves per second is called the **frequency.** One vibration per second is called one **Hertz** (Hz). This measurement is named for Heinrich Hertz, the German scientist who first showed that radio waves exist and are very similar to light waves.

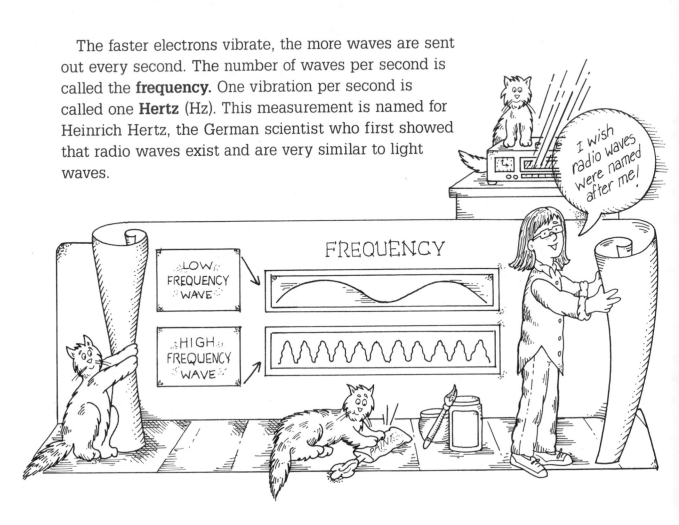

Try this...

Look at the AM dial of your radio. There are various numbers on the dial, ranging from about 530 to 1600. At one end of the dial there is usually the symbol kHZ. This stands for kiloHertz. (The prefix kilo means one thousand.) When you select 800 kHZ on the dial, for instance, this means that the radio wave you are receiving has a frequency of 800,000 vibrations per second.

Like all other waves, radio waves form peaks and valleys as they spread out. The distance between peaks is called the **wavelength**. Some wavelengths can be the length of a football field. Others can be only a few inches long.

Wavelength is usually measured in meters (1 meter equals 39.37 inches). On some radio dials you can read the wavelength of the radio waves as well as the frequency of their vibration.

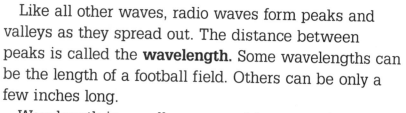

Try this...

Lightning creates radio waves. The next time there is an electrical storm, turn on your radio. Listen for the crackling sound you hear whenever there is a bolt of lightning. The radio waves produced by the lightning interfere with the waves produced by the normal broadcast.

15

In any one part of the country, dozens of radio stations are able to broadcast at the same time. They can do this because each station uses a different frequency and wavelength. This prevents the stations from interfering with each other. You can hear the program you want without getting it mixed up with some other station.

A government agency assigns a wavelength and frequency to every broadcasting station. This is the number you see on the radio dial that helps you locate your favorite station.

Try this...

You can make your own radio waves. Cut a piece of bell wire 1 foot long and strip the plastic covering off both ends. Tape one end to the bottom of a D cell. Move the battery near a radio that is turned on but tuned to a place on its dial where there is no program. Tap the top of the battery with the free end of the wire. Can you hear a "click" on the radio? The tiny sparks you are making are transmitting radio waves.

16

Transmitted waves are usually grouped together into **wave bands.** Two bands—one low frequency and one high frequency—are reserved for most common radio broadcasting. Television has its own band. Other bands are used only by police, airplanes, ships, and the military. One band, called CB, is even set aside for private citizens to use for doing business or just for chatting.

Try this...

Look at the FM band on your radio. Notice that the numbers on the dial range from about 88 to 108 MHz. (The prefix M stands for "Mega," which means million.) The frequencies in this band range from 88 million to 108 million vibrations per second.

17

BROADCASTING

From the outside, most radio stations look like ordinary offices. But on the door you will often see capital letters such as WQXR or KABC instead of a company name. These are the **call letters** that identify each station.

A tall mast or tower usually stands nearby. This is the transmitting antenna. Electric cables connect the antenna to the station. From this antenna the station broadcasts the radio waves that carry its programs.

Try this...

Look at the radio listings in the entertainment section of a newspaper. How many different radio stations are there? How many of these stations have you listened to?

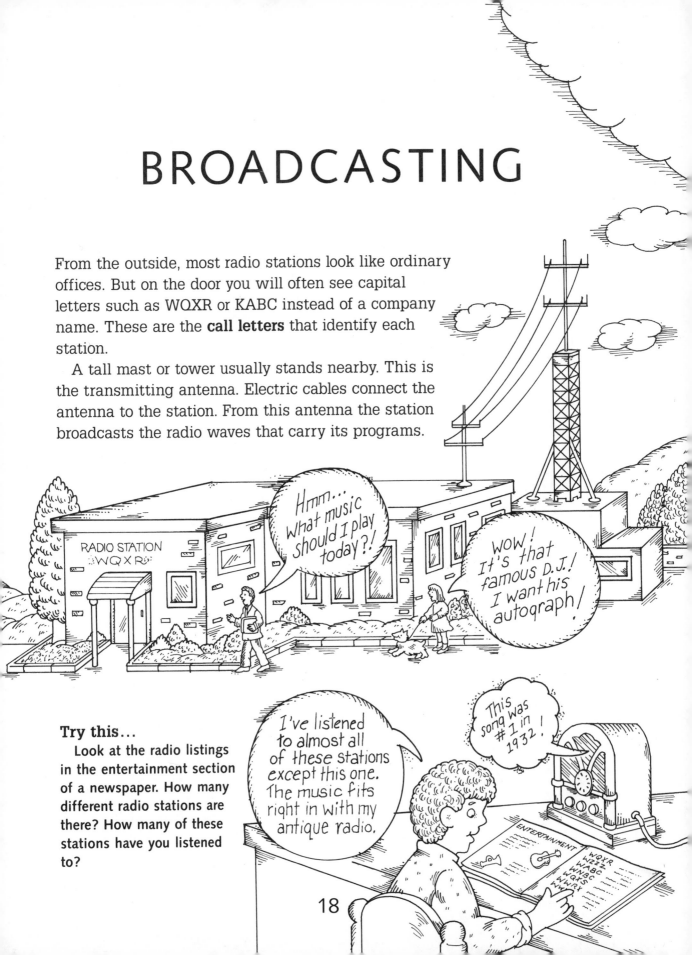

18

Some radio towers are 400 to 500 feet tall. The longer the wavelength, the taller the tower.

Try this…

Look at the strings of a piano. The low notes, the notes with a long wavelength, have long strings. The high notes, the notes with a short wavelength, have short strings. Although a radio antenna transmits radio waves instead of sound, it works in the same way. The shorter the wavelength, the shorter the antenna.

19

Most programs begin in the radio station's studio. This is a large room that holds several **microphones**. A microphone is an amazing instrument. It changes the sound patterns made by voices and musical instruments into matching electrical patterns. These patterns can then be sent out, riding on the radio waves.

The studio is usually soundproof, with glass walls that let the performers see what is going on outside without being disturbed by noise.

The sound engineer sits in the control room next to the studio. This person works the complicated dials and meters in front of him or her to make sure that the transmission is clear, and neither too loud nor too soft.

When musicians broadcast a concert, they sit in the studio and play into the microphone.

21

When you look at a microphone, all you really see is a cover with some holes in it. Inside, though, there is a thin metal disc called a diaphragm. Attached to the bottom of the diaphragm is a coil of wire. Near this coil of wire is a magnet.

When sound waves, or vibrations, pass through the holes and strike the diaphragm, the diaphragm also starts to vibrate. It vibrates in exactly the same patterns as the sound. In turn, the vibrations are passed on to the attached wire coil located near the magnet.

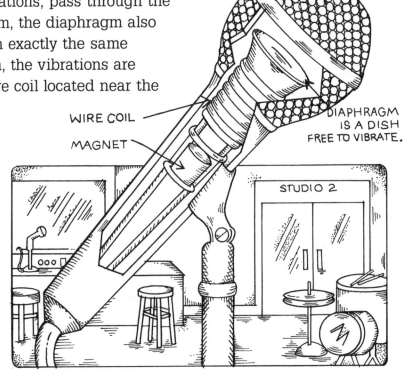

MICROPHONE

HOLES TO LET THE SOUND IN

WIRE COIL

MAGNET

DIAPHRAGM IS A DISH FREE TO VIBRATE.

STUDIO 2

Try this...

Blow up a balloon and tie the opening. Tune a radio to your favorite station and turn up the volume loud. Hold the balloon gently between your finger tips near the speaker of the radio. Feel the sound waves making the balloon vibrate.

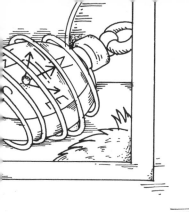

When a wire coil moves back and forth near a magnet, the wire becomes electrified. That's what happens in the microphone. As the coil vibrates, the electrons in the wire start to jump around. They copy the patterns of sound that are coming into the microphone and change them into patterns of electricity.

2.
SLIDE THE BAR MAGNET QUICKLY IN AND OUT OF THE WIRE COIL.

1.
TWIST THE STRIPPED ENDS OF WIRE TOGETHER.

ELECTRIFIED

Try this...

Cut a piece of bell wire 6 feet long and strip 1 inch of the plastic covering from each end. Near one end, wrap the wire six or seven turns around your hand to make a coil. Near the other end, wrap the wire six or seven turns around a compass. Connect the open ends by twisting them together. Now slide a bar magnet quickly in and out of the open coil. Can you see the compass needle jump? This tells you that you've made electricity flow through the wire.

I've seen enough art! what about you?

Yeah, me too! Gee, I wish I had my radio!

MAGNETIC!

23

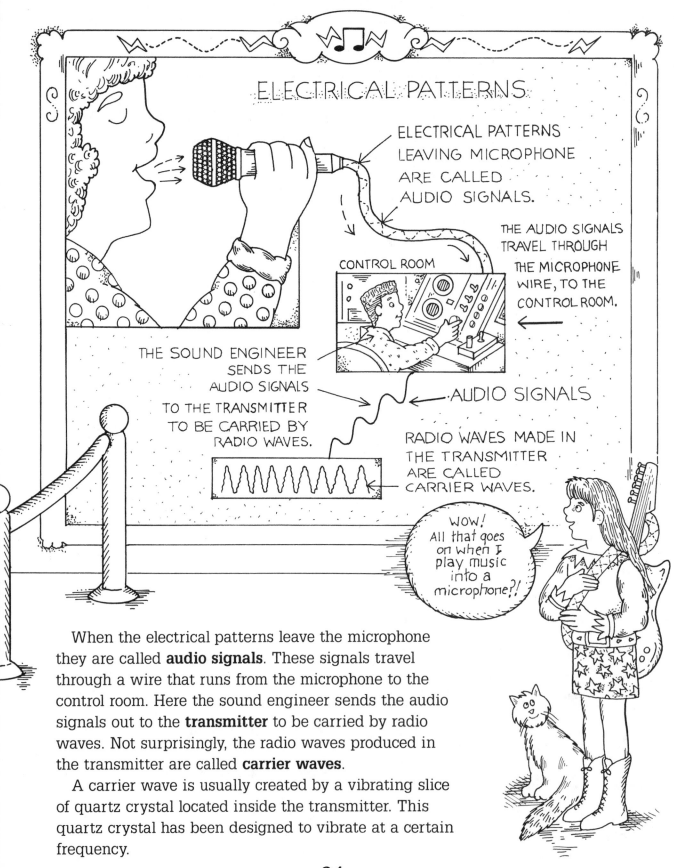

When the electrical patterns leave the microphone they are called **audio signals**. These signals travel through a wire that runs from the microphone to the control room. Here the sound engineer sends the audio signals out to the **transmitter** to be carried by radio waves. Not surprisingly, the radio waves produced in the transmitter are called **carrier waves**.

A carrier wave is usually created by a vibrating slice of quartz crystal located inside the transmitter. This quartz crystal has been designed to vibrate at a certain frequency.

24

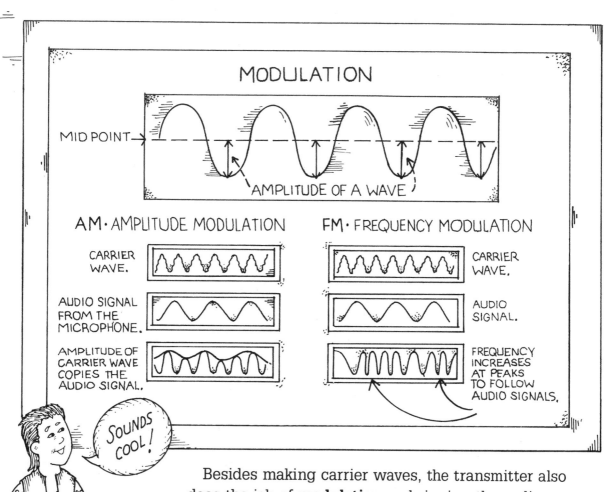

MODULATION

MID POINT →

AMPLITUDE OF A WAVE

AM · AMPLITUDE MODULATION

CARRIER WAVE.

AUDIO SIGNAL FROM THE MICROPHONE.

AMPLITUDE OF CARRIER WAVE COPIES THE AUDIO SIGNAL.

FM · FREQUENCY MODULATION

CARRIER WAVE.

AUDIO SIGNAL.

FREQUENCY INCREASES AT PEAKS TO FOLLOW AUDIO SIGNALS.

SOUNDS COOL!

GREAT!

Besides making carrier waves, the transmitter also does the job of **modulation**, or bringing the audio signal and the carrier wave together. Remember, each radio station must broadcast at a specific wavelength and frequency. So, one kind of modulation changes the size, or **amplitude**, of the wave being transmitted. This is called **amplitude modulation**, or **AM**. Another kind of modulation makes small changes in the frequency of the carrier wave. This is called **frequency modulation**, or **FM**.

FM gets rid of the crackling noises called *static* and makes the reception very clear. But the range of FM is limited. Usually, FM antennas are placed on the roofs of tall buildings to give them a wider range.

After the carrier waves are modulated, an electronic amplifier gives them extra power. At last, they rush to the transmitting antenna. And from there they radiate out into the air, where your radio can pick them up.

25

LET'S LOOK
INSIDE YOUR RADIO

Day and night, hour after hour, radio waves are criss-crossing through the air. They travel all around you—and even right through you—whether you're out of doors or inside. But the only way you can detect them and hear their messages is by turning on a radio.

The radio receives the signals carried on radio waves and translates them back into sounds. That's why we often call it a **receiver**.

RADIO STATION WXRS

I don't <u>feel</u> a thing!

This song will go right through you. ♪♫

A look inside your radio would show you dozens of little colored cylinders, discs, and glass tubes. These are the electronic parts of the radio. They have technical names such as **transistors, capacitors, resistors,** and **vacuum tubes**; and they are arranged in working units called **circuits.** Each circuit does a specific job, but they all work together to bring you your favorite programs.

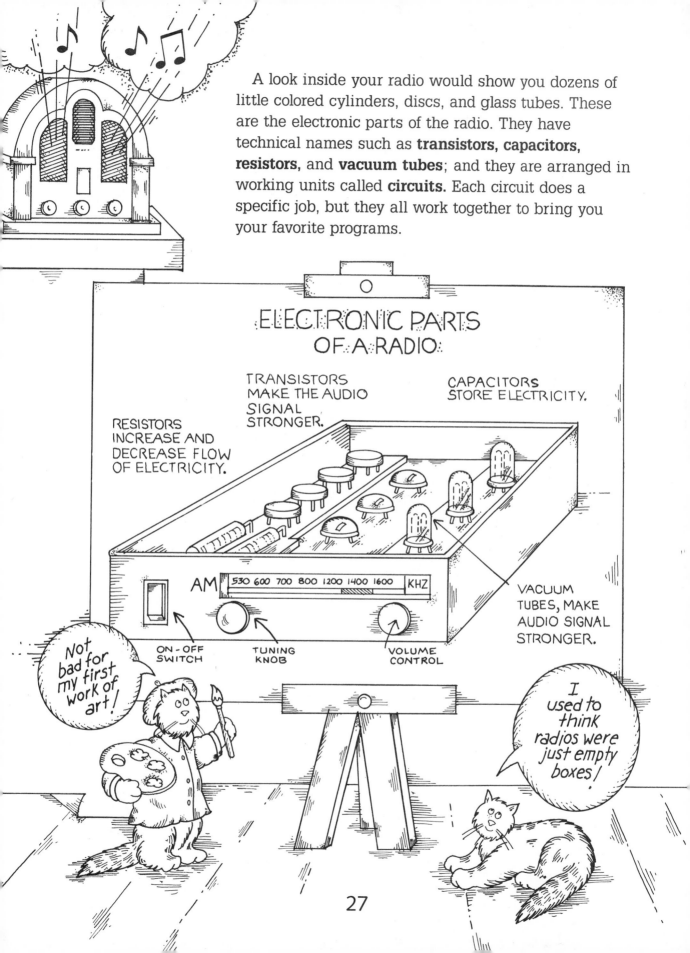

ELECTRONIC PARTS
OF A RADIO

TRANSISTORS MAKE THE AUDIO SIGNAL STRONGER.

CAPACITORS STORE ELECTRICITY.

RESISTORS INCREASE AND DECREASE FLOW OF ELECTRICITY.

AM   530 600 700 800 1200 1400 1600   KHZ

VACUUM TUBES, MAKE AUDIO SIGNAL STRONGER.

ON - OFF SWITCH

TUNING KNOB

VOLUME CONTROL

Not bad for my first work of art!

I used to think radios were just empty boxes!

27

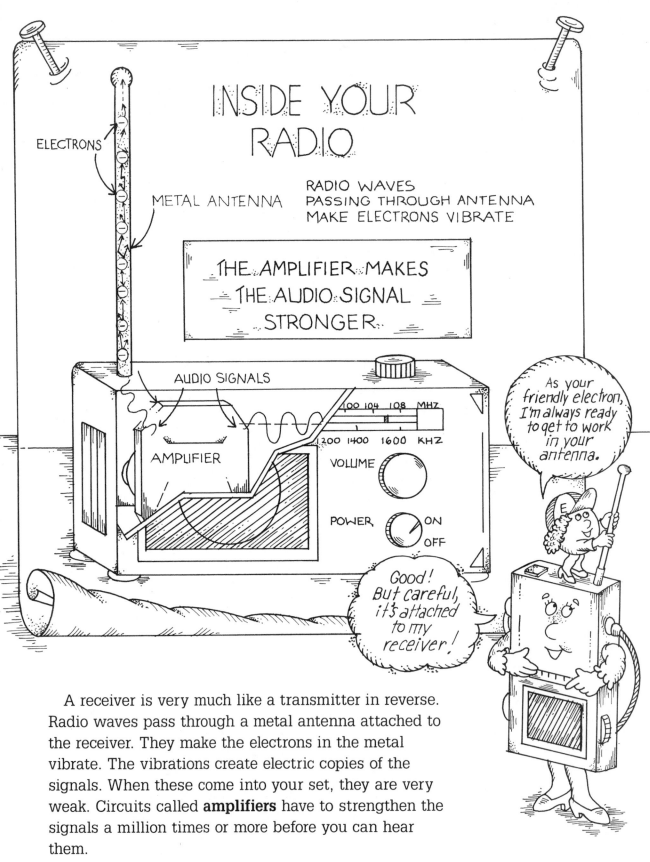

A receiver is very much like a transmitter in reverse. Radio waves pass through a metal antenna attached to the receiver. They make the electrons in the metal vibrate. The vibrations create electric copies of the signals. When these come into your set, they are very weak. Circuits called **amplifiers** have to strengthen the signals a million times or more before you can hear them.

As soon as you turn on your radio, the electricity coming in brings the right amount of power to all the working circuits. The first thing you must do is pick out the station you want. To do this you use the *tuning control.* It moves a pointer along a numbered scale. When you place the pointer opposite 800 kHz, for example, you are choosing a radio station with a carrier frequency of 800,000 Hertz. The radio has to find this wavelength or frequency from among dozens of others that are passing through the antenna. The circuit that does this job is called the **tuner**.

Now the radio wave that you just picked has to be decoded. A circuit called the **detector** separates the audio signals from the carrier wave. It discards the carrier wave and sends the sound signals to be *amplified,* or given more power. The volume dial on your radio helps you control the strength of the sound you want. Finally, the job of the *loudspeaker* is to change the electrical signals back into sounds you can hear as words or music.

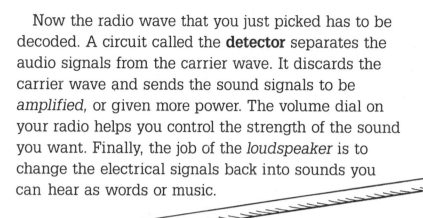

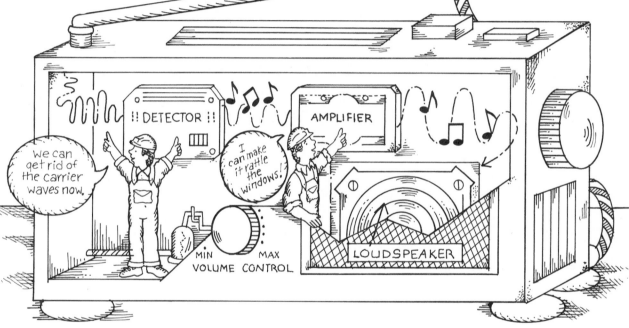

Try this...

Fold a piece of wax paper over a comb. Put your lips gently against the paper and hum a song. The sound waves made by your voice cause the paper to vibrate. Feel the vibrations on your lips, and listen to the way they amplify your voice.

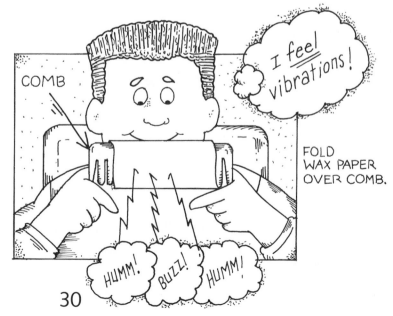

LOUDSPEAKER

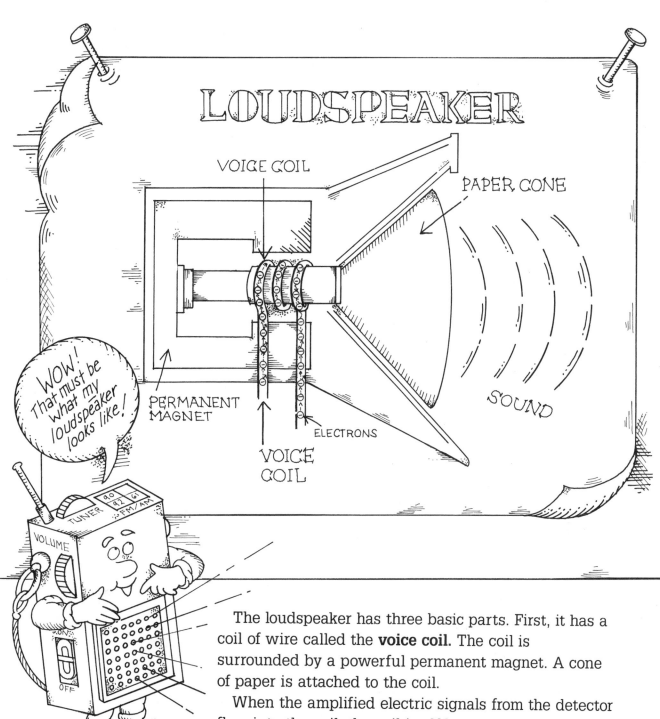

VOICE COIL

PAPER CONE

PERMANENT MAGNET

ELECTRONS

VOICE COIL

SOUND

WOW! That must be what my loudspeaker looks like!

TUNER

FM/AM

VOLUME

ON

OFF

The loudspeaker has three basic parts. First, it has a coil of wire called the **voice coil.** The coil is surrounded by a powerful permanent magnet. A cone of paper is attached to the coil.

When the amplified electric signals from the detector flow into the coil, the coil itself becomes magnetic. The permanent magnet attracts and moves the magnetized coil. This coil responds to the patterns of the audio signal and vibrates back and forth. It shakes the paper cone. And the air vibrations caused by the paper are the sounds you hear when you turn on the radio.

31

TOY CARS
AND TELESCOPES

Only a hundred years ago, radio waves were a
scientific novelty. Today, they are part of our daily lives
in dozens of ways. For one thing, without radio there
would be no television. It is radio waves that carry
video signals as well as audio signals. *Video* refers to
things you can see, *audio* refers to things you can hear.
Together they bring you the programs you love to
watch on your TV set.

Radio waves also help you talk to friends who live far away by radiotelephone. Long distance calls are often carried part of the way by radio waves. The waves can take your call across rugged country or large bodies of water without the use of wires or cables. The radio waves that carry your phone call part of the way through the air are high frequency waves called **microwaves**.

33

Microwaves cannot travel much beyond the horizon, because they cannot bend around the curve of the earth. To reach very long distances, microwaves have to be passed on by a series of relays—high towers that receive the signals and rebroadcast them.

Mobile telephones use the same system. You often see people telephoning in their car, on the beach, or in their garden. To carry calls across the oceans, satellites are often used as relay stations floating high above the earth.

Many people get in touch with each other directly, using small portable transmitters and receivers, such as walkie-talkies and beepers. The government has set aside a band of frequencies called the **citizens' band**, or **CB**, for such uses. More powerful CB radios in trucks and cars help many drivers exchange information about road and traffic conditions as they are traveling.

Try this...

See if you can find any radio amateurs, or *hams*, listed in the white pages of your phone book. Look under *Radio, Amateur*. These hobbyists often build their own radios, have their own call letters, and talk to other hams all over the world.

35

Radio waves are also used to gather information about the world around us. Planes and ships use them for navigation. For example, a ship sends out radio waves that "echo" back from nearby objects. The pattern of echoes forms a picture that shows hazards such as rocks or other ships. This important civilian and military use of radio is called **radar** (*radio detection and ranging*).

Try this...
Most "remote control" gadgets use radio. The toy cars that seem to zoom around on their own are an example. Can you make a list of others?

Many stars emit energy in the form of radio waves. Astronomers pick up these waves with huge dish-shaped antennas called radio telescopes. In this way they have been able to identify hundreds of new starlike objects in space.

Nowadays, environmental scientists depend on information radioed from balloons floating high above the earth. The automatic measuring instruments in these balloons radio back data that help us predict changes in climate and weather.

So many uses of radio are crowding the space around us that the Federal Communications Commission (FCC) may soon put stricter limits on broadcasting. What a change from 1901, when the first radio signal reached the untouched airwaves of North America!

GLOSSARY

AM (Amplitude Modulation)—a way of adding sound signals to a carrier wave by changing its amplitude, or height.

Amplifier (AM-pli-fy-ur)—an electronic circuit that increases the size of radio and audio signals.

Amplitude (AM-plih-tood)—the height of a wave.

Antenna (an-TEN-uh)—a metal rod or wire for receiving or sending radio signals.

Audio signals (AU-de-oh SIG-nul)—electrical wave pattern created by sound.

Call letters—The letters that identify a radio station.

Capacitor (kuh-PASS-i-tur)—an electronic circuit element that stores electricity.

Carrier wave—The radio wave that carries the sound signal from transmitter to receiver.

CB (Citizens' Band)—the set of radio frequencies reserved for use by private citizens.

Detector (di-TEK-tur)—a circuit that separates the sound signal from the carrier waves.

Electron (uh-LEK-trahn)—one of the basic building blocks that make up all matter.

FM (Frequency Modulation)—a way of adding sound signals to the carrier wave by changing its frequency.

Frequency (FREE-kwen-see)—the number of waves per second sent out by a radio transmitter.

Ham—a radio hobbyist who operates his or her own radio station.

Hertz—a unit of frequency equal to one vibration per second. Named after German scientist Heinrich Hertz.

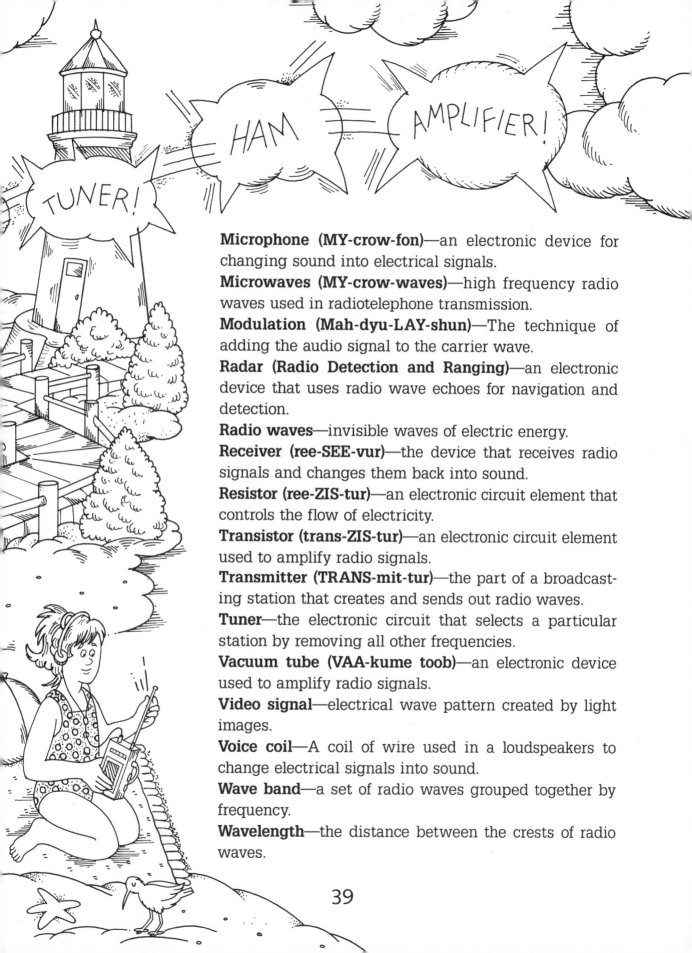

Microphone (MY-crow-fon)—an electronic device for changing sound into electrical signals.

Microwaves (MY-crow-waves)—high frequency radio waves used in radiotelephone transmission.

Modulation (Mah-dyu-LAY-shun)—The technique of adding the audio signal to the carrier wave.

Radar (Radio Detection and Ranging)—an electronic device that uses radio wave echoes for navigation and detection.

Radio waves—invisible waves of electric energy.

Receiver (ree-SEE-vur)—the device that receives radio signals and changes them back into sound.

Resistor (ree-ZIS-tur)—an electronic circuit element that controls the flow of electricity.

Transistor (trans-ZIS-tur)—an electronic circuit element used to amplify radio signals.

Transmitter (TRANS-mit-tur)—the part of a broadcasting station that creates and sends out radio waves.

Tuner—the electronic circuit that selects a particular station by removing all other frequencies.

Vacuum tube (VAA-kume toob)—an electronic device used to amplify radio signals.

Video signal—electrical wave pattern created by light images.

Voice coil—A coil of wire used in a loudspeakers to change electrical signals into sound.

Wave band—a set of radio waves grouped together by frequency.

Wavelength—the distance between the crests of radio waves.

39

INDEX